The GREAT ALL-TIME EXCUSE BOOK

by **MAUREEN KUSHNER**

ILLUSTRATED by **Sanford Hoffman**

Sterling Publishing Co., Inc.   New York

This book is for Felix and the Cat

A Special
Willowisp Press, Inc.
Edition

Library of Congress Cataloging-in-Publication Data

Kushner, Maureen.
 The great all-time excuse book / by Maureen Kushner ;
illustrated by Sanford Hoffman.
  p. cm.
 Summary: Hundreds of wacky excuses to use in familiar
situations at school, at home, and in the neighborhood.
 1. Excuses—Juvenile humor. 2. Wit and humor, Juvenile.
[1. Excuses—Wit and humor. 2. Wit and humor.]
I. Hoffman, Sanford, ill. II. Title.
PN6231.E87K88 1990
818′.5402—dc20   89-49403
                                                       CIP
                                                       AC

10 9 8 7 6 5 4

First paperback edition published in 1991 by
Sterling Publishing Company, Inc.
387 Park Avenue South, New York, N.Y. 10016
Text © 1990 by Maureen Kushner
Illustrations © 1990 by Sterling Publishing Co.
Distributed in Canada by Sterling Publishing
% Canadian Manda Group, P.O. Box 920, Station U
Toronto, Ontario, Canada M8Z 5P9
Distributed in Great Britain and Europe by Cassell PLC
Villiers House, 41/47 Strand, London WC2N 5JE, England
Distributed in Australia by Capricorn Ltd.
P.O. Box 665, Lane Cove, NSW 2066
Manufactured in the United States of America
All rights reserved

ISBN 0-87406-624-7

CONTENTS

EXCUSES, EXCUSES!

Excuse me.

Why? Did you sneeze?

No, but excuse me anyway.

What for?

Just in case I don't have the right excuse.

Why do you need an excuse? You didn't do anything.

That's just when you *do* need an excuse.

When you didn't do anything?

Of course. People are always blaming you when it's not your fault.

That's true.

And that's why you need this book.

Why? What's this book going to do for me?

This book is going to get you away from all the boring excuses that everyone's heard over and over. It's going to give you new excuses—funny ones, wacky ones—ones that will crack your friends up and drive your teachers nuts.

**I guess I could use a few new excuses.
Do you have one for why I didn't
clean my room?**

 Yes, we've got a few.

Or why I didn't take the garbage out?

Sure, we have some good ones.

Or why I got a rotten report card?

 Excuse me.

Why?

I can't stand around here jabbering. The next
Ice Age is coming.

It is?

 My molecules are being rearranged.

They are?

I've got to go shopping.

You do?

My goldfish is flying in from Mars and I have to
pick her up.

 You're putting me on!

Well, excuse me!

Chapter 1

SCHOOL—GO SLOW

Why did you bring your dog in here?

Shh—this is my cat. He only thinks he's my dog.

What's that on your desk?

Nuclear fallout.

An abstract replica of Mount Everest.

Recycled spitballs from the Environment
  Committee.

A food sample from the cafeteria I'm
  analyzing for science class.

**Why are you writing with your left hand
when you told me you're a rightie?**

I was writing a left-handed compliment.

I screwed my arms on backwards this
morning.

I wasn't in the right mood.

I woke up on the wrong
side of the bed.

Why don't you ever pay attention?

I did once and it wouldn't pay me back.

It doesn't take credit cards.

I never got a bill.

How much do I have to pay it?

Why do you always daydream during math?

That isn't daydreaming! It's a post-hypnotic trance.

Because I forgot to do it during social studies.

Is this math class? I thought it was still Penmanship.

I wasn't daydreaming. I was working a problem out in my head.

I wasn't daydreaming. I was having an out-of-body experience.

I'm doing geometry. I'm thinking about the Bermuda Triangle.

I'm doing arithmetic. I'm figuring out how many shopping days till Christmas.

What happened to your pencil?

This isn't a pencil. It's an overweight toothpick with a giant zit.

Oh, this is a Christmas present from my termite.

The pencil sharpener went into a feeding frenzy.

This isn't a pencil. It's petrified beef jerky.

Chapter 2

CLASS COME TO ORDER!

Why do you always squeak the chalk?

I'm sending messages in Mouse Code.

Why are you writing on the blackboard?

Because I can't reach the ceiling.

'Cause I'm bored of education!

The paper isn't big enough to hold all my thoughts.

Because you told me not to write on the floor.

It's got more space than my notebook.

Why don't you answer my question?

Didn't you tell me not to answer back?

Did you ever hear of the Fifth
Amendment?

I'm waiting for the multiple choice.

My answer is none of the above.

I'm saving my answers for *Jeopardy*.

Don't you ever stop talking?

Stop Talking? Stop it from what?

I'm not talking—I'm practising word-processing.

Well, talk is cheap and I can't afford anything better.

My lips keep coming unzipped.

Where's Talking going?

I had alphabet soup for lunch and words keep coming out of my mouth.

I don't know—I'm not listening.

Why are you calling out?

Would you prefer that I telephone?

I didn't know how to call in.

That was my inner voice struggling to be heard.

I was an auctioneer in a former life.

These shoes are new and they're killing me.

It's cheaper than sending a singing telegram.

21

Why are you raising your hand when I asked everyone to wait until I finished the story?

I'm not! I'm testing out my new
  deodorant.

I'm not! I'm drying my nail polish.

I'm not! I'm unscrewing my arm.

I'm not! I'm swatting flies.

I'm not! I'm hailing a cab.

I'm not! I'm clearing the air.

I'm not! I'm holding up the ceiling.

What are you doing crawling around the floor?

I wanted to get to the bottom of things.

Just getting down to the nitty-gritty.

I was actually crawling on the ceiling, but I fell off.

Chapter 3

WHAT ARE YOU DOING?

Why aren't you folding your hands?

I thought you don't have to pray in school.

I folded my paper. Isn't that enough?

I thought it would count if I just crossed my fingers.

Why are you scribbling all over your desk?

I'm not. I'm writing neatly.

I'm not. I'm just adding my name to the list of other great people who sat here.

I'm not. I'm just answering some of the personals.

I ran out of paper.

I was following orders. Didn't you say, "Mark my word?"

Why are you standing on the desk?

Because I don't know how to stand on my
   head.

I'm trying to upgrade my image.

I'm preparing for a summit conference.

I like to stay on top of things.

I'm above average in everything.

I was set up.

I function on a very high level.

29

**Why did you throw the paper airplane out
the window?**

I was feeling space-y.

You said to get rid of it.

Because it doesn't have an automatic launcher.

I was testing a new way to do my paper route.

I wanted to join the jet set.

I was giving my pet ant a free ride.

I was too tired to carry it home.

What paper airplane? That was Flight 905 to Daytona.

Why were you absent from school yesterday?

I wasn't absent. I was temporarily invisible.

Absence is my only A.

I wanted to see if the class could survive without me.

So the room wouldn't be overcrowded.

Because absence makes the heart grow fonder.

Chapter 4

WHAT'S THE MATTER WITH YOU?

Did you get sunburned?

No—I'm just an unusually bright kid.

Why do you keep running around the room?

My nose is the only thing that's running. The rest of me is just trying to keep up.

I'm standing still. The room is running around me.

The doctor told me not to get run down.

I'm part of the human race, aren't I?

I'm trying to find where it begins.

I'm practising for a career on the merry-go-round.

Are you thirsty again?

No, I'm Friday.

No, I'm filling my waterbed.

No, I'm about to fill the swimming pool.

No, my room is on fire and I'm just going
to put it out.

No, I'm going to take a bath.

Why are you putting on lipstick in class?

I'm getting ready for my make-up exam.

I'm trying to make it easy for my voice to find its way out of my mouth.

This is my ecology homework. I'm beautifying the environment.

Why did you push me?

Because you're a pushy kid.

I was too tired to pull you.

Because there wasn't anyone else around to push.

I thought you wanted to get ahead in life.

Why do you always pull my hair?

I like to get to the root of things.

Is that what it is—I thought it was
  linguine with clam sauce.

It's too hard to push it.

Just hunting for endangered species.

I'll stop—I don't want to upset the
  ecological balance.

I thought maybe your brush was stuck in
  there.

**Is that a new ring
on your finger?**

No, it's a bracelet that
shrank at the
cleaners.

No, it's a lifesaver I'm
saving for after lunch.

Yes, the one in the bathtub didn't fit.

No, it's a Cheerio. Got some milk?

42

Why don't you listen when I talk to you?

I am listening. Don't you see me
yawning?

Sorry—I thought your ventriloquist was
doing the talking.

I can either listen to you talk or watch you
dribble, but I can't do both.

Oh, excuse me—I thought you
were talking in your sleep.

Why are you showing off your dimples?

They're not dimples. I just had my face
pierced.

Oh, they're just places where I hide my
chewing gum.

What dimples? Those are inverted
pimples.

Chapter 5

WHY DID YOU DO IT?

Did you tear your pants?

No, that's my built-in air conditioner.

Why did you get a zero on your test?

That's not a zero—it's a moon. The teacher ran out of stars.

That's not a zero—it's a racetrack for fleas.

That's not a zero—it's a picture of Cyclops' eye.

That's not a zero—it's the 15th letter of the alphabet. My teacher couldn't re-member the other ones.

Why didn't you take the garbage out?

It never takes me out.

We're not interested in the same things.

I had another date.

It's hard to dance with a Hefty bag.

It just wouldn't be home without it.

The tooth fairy offered me a better deal.

I'm too attached to my teeth.

Drills are boring!

Because he always chews me out.

I think children should be seen and not
  hurt.

He always takes my gum.

Why didn't you see the doctor when you were supposed to?

Every time I see him my tongue gets depressed.

I did see him—but I don't remember where.

I saw him—Dr. Huxtable on TV!

'Cause he tells sick jokes.

Because he loses his patients.

Why didn't you tell us you got your report card?

I thought I had the right to remain silent.

I needed time to appeal to the Supreme Court.

I'm not taking any chances now that capital punishment is legal again.

What happened to your brains today?

The dentist drilled too deep.

I blew my nose too hard.

I was being brainwashed and they went
down the drain.

Chapter 6

WHAT'S NEW?

Are you gaining weight?

No, your eyes are just getting smaller.

No, you shrank my clothes.

That's a heavy question.

Are you moving?

No, just trying to keep a step ahead of the
  police.

No, I've always lived in that truck.

No, I miss all this stuff when I go to
  school, so today I'm taking it with me.

Why do you still bite your nails?

My fingers are too long.

They taste better than nuts and bolts.

I'm on a high protein diet.

I don't. They just get worn down from
   scratching my head.

My toenails are too hard to reach.

Are you cutting the grass now?

No, I'm feeding my pet lawn mower.

No, this is an outdoor vacuum cleaner.

Did you go to the supermarket again?

No, I'm walking my
shopping cart.

No, all this food just came
in the mail.

Are you going swimming again?

No, just going to wash the lint out of my
bellybutton.

No, I'm checking to see if the oysters I
planted last year have grown any pearls.

No, I just want to find out if I have drip-
dry skin.

No, I'm just getting ready for the swimsuit
competition.

Are you going skiing?

No, I'm carrying chopsticks for the Jolly
   Green Giant.

No, I'm laying a railroad track.

No, these are just the rabbit ears for my
   new TV.

Is that a surfboard?

Surfboard?
This is an
ironing board
for bikinis.

No, it's a starched
beach blanket.

No, it's a tongue depressor for my pet
shark.

Is that a tennis racket?

No, I use this to paddle my canoe.

No, this is a giant fly swatter.

No, this is my Abominable Snowshoe.

Why did your baseball team lose?

We were way off base.

The coach turned into a pumpkin.

Everyone went batty.

Chapter 7

EATING IT UP

Why are you hiccuping?

I'm not. This is an epiglottal seizure.

I swallowed a beeper.

I just ate franks and
   Mexican jumping
   beans.

Why aren't you eating the school lunch?

I take poison at home, thank you.

School lunch? I thought this was leftovers from chemistry class.

I left my gas mask at home.

I'm waiting for the Board of Health to analyze it.

I ate some of it last year, but now it's getting stale.

Why are you eating with your fingers?

I'm not. I'm putting my fingers in my
    mouth.

Would you rather I ate with your fingers?

I tried eating with my baseball mitt, but I
    couldn't get the food into my mouth.

It's neater than eating with my toes.

It beats eating with my elbows.

Can you imagine eating without them?

'Cause I'm hungry.

72

No, but you never know when you'll meet
  an Indian wrestler.

No, I was just afraid the lunch tray was
  going to blow away.

No, I was holding up my chin.

Yes, I try to be symmetrical.

No, sometimes I keep them in a big box.

Only when I'm eating them with tomato
  sauce.

Is the food too spicy?

No, smoke always comes out of my ears.

No, but I think my hair has just become
   naturally curly.

I'll tell you when I stop crying.

Chapter 8

HEY, YOU!

Why aren't you with your class?

That's classified information.

I'm in a class by myself.

Is that my kite?

No—it's a stingray on a leash.

No, I'm trying to catch a flying fish.

No, I'm just drying my laundry
   piece by piece.

Why are you such a big pest?

I started out being a little pest, but
practice makes perfect.

Am I really a pest? I was trying to be more
of a general nuisance.

Sheer talent, I guess!

It's my mother's fault. She called the
exterminator but I was outside playing.

Why are you wearing glasses?

I like making a spectacle of myself.

I use these hooks to keep my face attached to the rest of my head.

I'm planning to do some sightseeing.

I have to. They keep my eyeballs from falling out.

Why are you standing on your head?

Would you rather I stand on *your* head?

I'm trying to get the dust-balls out of my pockets.

That's funny. I thought it was the room that was upside down.

Because your head is too far off the ground.

I'm giving my brains a workout.

No, I always dribble after lunch.

No, actually I thought I was doing the
   backstroke.

No, baseball. Isn't that home plate up
   there on the backboard?

No, I'm checking the ceiling for cobwebs.

No, I thought I was playing golf, but I
   can't find the first hole.

Why are you always fighting?

I'm wrestling with that question.

It must be these boxer shorts I'm wearing.

Beats me.

Chapter 9

GO TO YOUR ROOM!

Are you sneezing?

No, this is how we say "Hello" in Martian.

The label says wash and wear.

My designer is Jacques Cousteau.

I ran out of quarters for the dryer.

I just finished walking my pet fish.

I'm wishy-washy.

I didn't fit in the dryer.

Why didn't you close the door?

There's a mosquito in here with
claustrophobia.

I'm waiting for Santa Claus.

Because I have an open mind.

Because we're such a close-knit family.

I'm expecting a friend who knows too many knock-knocks.

Because there's a sabre-tooth tiger in the house.

Because my poltergeist would get lonely.

What's this candy doing in your bed?

I wanted to have sweet dreams.

It's not candy. It's medicine for my sweet tooth.

Getting a little bit of rest.

That's a sticky subject.

I thought it was a tasteful decoration.

Don't ask me. I gave it a good licking and sent it home.

Why don't you make your bed?

And disturb all the crumbs?

The dog's still in it.

I'm not a carpenter.

90

Why are your toys all over the floor?

Ask them. I told them to stay in their box.

They're all wound up.

I don't know. It must be some kind of convention.

Roger Rabbit must be casting his next movie.

A toynado hit them.

Why don't you turn off the lights?

I'm a light sleeper.

Watt?

You got me. I'm completely in the dark.

I was trying to trap a killer moth.

Didn't you tell me you invested in energy
   stocks?

I'm conserving solar energy.

I didn't want to wear out the switch.

I'd only have to turn them on again.

The last time I turned off the light, I
   couldn't find the way out.

Why don't you clean your room?

My room? I thought it was my closet.

I couldn't find it.

Mr. Clean was always cleaning his room and what did he get to show for it but a bald head?

We ran out of Kleenex.

I did clean it. It just got dirty again.

Because it's not Leap Year.

INDEX